BEST
SIMPLE
SUPPERS
FOR TWO

BEST
SIMPLE
SUPPERS
FOR TWO

FAST AND FOOLPROOF RECIPES
FOR ONE, TWO, OR A FEW

LAURA ARNOLD

THE COUNTRYMAN PRESS

A DIVISION OF W. W. NORTON & COMPANY

INDEPENDENT PUBLISHERS SINCE 1923

For information about permission to reproduce selections from this book, write to Permissions, The Countryman Press, 500 Fifth Avenue, New York, NY 10110

For information about special discounts for bulk purchases, please contact W. W. Norton Special Sales at specialsales@wwnorton.com or 800-233-4830

Library of Congress Cataloging-in-Publication Data

Names: Arnold, Laura, author.
Title: Best simple suppers for two : fast and foolproof recipes for one, two, or a few / Laura Arnold.
Description: New York, NY : Countryman Press, a division of W. W. Norton & Company, Independent Publishers Since 1923, [2017] | Includes index.
Identifiers: LCCN 2016058131 | ISBN 9781682680360 (pbk.)
Subjects: LCSH: Quick and easy cooking. | Cooking for two. | LCGFT: Cookbooks.
Classification: LCC TX833.5 .A76 2017 | DDC 641.5/12—dc23 LC record available at https://lccn.loc.gov/2016058131

The Countryman Press
www.countrymanpress.com

A division of W. W. Norton & Company
500 Fifth Avenue, New York, NY 10110
www.wwnorton.com

1 2 3 4 5 6 7 8 9 0

FOR MY MOM—
THANKS FOR BEING
THE SOUS-CHEF OF MY LIFE

BEST SIMPLE SUPPERS FOR TWO
CONTENTS

Chapter Three: Seafood / 69

Chapter Four: Vegetarian / 81

Chapter Five: One-Pot Meals / 99

Introduction

Whether it's date night, you're having a friend over for dinner, or you're cooking for you and your roommate, cooking for two comes up all the time. The only problem is that most recipes yield four to six servings. Not only does this make cooking more expensive, but it leads to leftovers when you may prefer to have none. *Best Simple Suppers for Two* solves these problems by providing quick, easy dinners for two, designed to get you in the kitchen without the cost, hassle, and time of cooking a four- to six-person meal.

Even better, cooking for two is fun and can bring friends and couples into the kitchen to share time together. This book provides recipes that are just as effortless as ordering takeout or going to a restaurant. It is possible to get dinner on the table on a Tuesday evening after a stressful day at work because these simple, fast, and easy recipes allow you to cook a meal in less than an hour. On the weekend, date night becomes a shared experience in the kitchen, a time when you can learn how to make a healthier and cheaper meal at home.

These five basic chapters make it easy for you to find a recipe that will satisfy your cravings. Hungry for chicken? Try Quick Roasted Chicken Thighs with Garlic Potatoes. Or shrimp? Try the Shrimp Salad Roll. Several recipes also call for only one pan or pot, which makes cleaning a dream! Cooking for two can be simple as well as fun.

It is not only cooking for two that's essential—so is cooking for one. And cooking for one is always a challenge. Immediate questions come into my head when I am cooking for myself—how much food should I buy? Am I really going to eat all of these leftovers? What if I just want to make two servings of this recipe that serves eight people? These are all common problems that come with cooking for yourself. When you make these recipes for one, you get to cook once and eat twice, which I find to be the perfect compromise. One serving of leftovers comes in handy during any given week. You also won't break the bank by buying excess ingredients. So get in the kitchen and make a home-cooked meal in the same amount of time it would take to order takeout, but at half the price.

Ingredients and Equipment

The recipes in this book are simple and easy. As a result, the amount of ingredients is fewer than the amount you would need for a normal recipe. This book was designed to use similar spices, produce, and proteins in multiple recipes so that you can shop once and then cook two to three different meals. With that in mind, you can look for similar recipes throughout the book when meal planning for the week. This will keep your costs down and also minimize food waste.

The cooking equipment you need for these recipes is not complicated. Regular-sized cooking equipment is fine even though the amounts of ingredients are quartered or halved in these recipes for two. Equipment that is essential for cooking with this book:

- Cast-iron skillets, 8-inch, and 10- or 12-inch
- 8-inch square baking dish
- Sauté pan and nonstick sauté pan
- Grill or grill pan (preferred, but you can use a cast-iron skillet instead)
- Large pot

Most important, have fun and enjoy your time in the kitchen!

CHAPTER ONE
SALADS

Grilled Corn Fiesta Salad

Grill any fresh veggie to add to the salad for new flavor!

Prep time: 15 minutes   Cook time: 15 minutes

FOR THE SALAD

2 ears corn, shucked

½ bunch scallions

1 pint cherry tomatoes, halved

One 15-ounce can black beans, drained and rinsed

1 head romaine lettuce, thinly sliced

⅓ cup cotija cheese, crumbled

2 avocados, pitted, peeled, and diced

¼ cup cilantro leaves, roughly chopped

Tortilla chips, crushed, for serving

FOR THE DRESSING

1 lime, juiced

2 teaspoons honey

½ teaspoon cumin

⅓ cup olive oil

1 teaspoon kosher salt

½ teaspoon freshly ground black pepper

To make the salad: Preheat the grill or a grill pan over medium-high heat. Add the corn and the scallions and lightly char on all sides, 3 to 5 minutes per side. Remove from the grill and allow to cool slightly. Cut the kernels off the cob and thinly slice the scallions. Place the kernels and scallions in a large bowl. Add the cherry tomatoes, black beans, lettuce, cheese, avocado, and cilantro to the bowl.

To make the dressing: Add the lime juice, honey, and cumin to a small bowl and whisk to combine. While whisking, slowly drizzle in the olive oil. Season with salt and pepper and whisk again. Drizzle the dressing around the outside of the salad and toss to combine. Serve the tortilla chips over the top of the salad.

Caprese Salad with Basil Pesto

Turn this salad into a great sandwich by putting the ingredients on toasted thick crusty bread like Italian ciabatta.

Prep time: 10 minutes   Cook time: 5 minutes

FOR THE SALAD

One 16-ounce ball fresh mozzarella

2 large ripe tomatoes

⅓ cup fresh basil leaves, torn into pieces

3 tablespoons olive oil

½ bunch chives, thinly sliced, for garnish

½ teaspoon flaky sea salt or kosher salt

½ teaspoon freshly ground black pepper

Crusty bread, toasted, for serving

FOR THE PESTO

½ cup store-bought pesto

¼ cup fresh basil leaves, torn into pieces

1 lemon, zested

½ teaspoon kosher salt

½ teaspoon freshly ground black pepper

To make the salad: Slice the mozzarella and tomatoes into ¼- to ½-inch thick slices. Alternate the slices of mozzarella and tomatoes on a plate. Wedge the basil in between the mozzarella and tomato slices. Drizzle with olive oil, garnish with chives, and season with salt and pepper.

To make the pesto: Combine the prepared pesto, basil leaves, and lemon zest in a bowl. Season with salt and pepper. Serve the salad with the pesto on the side and plenty of toasted crusty bread.

Watermelon Salad with Feta & Mint

To add a new dimension of flavor, grill the watermelon for 3 minutes on each side.

Total time: 10 minutes

FOR THE SALAD

1 baby seedless watermelon, cut into 1-inch cubes

½ cup feta cheese, crumbled

¼ cup mint leaves, large leaves torn into pieces

3 tablespoons chives, thinly sliced

One 5-ounce box baby arugula

½ teaspoon kosher salt

FOR THE DRESSING

2 tablespoons red wine vinegar

¼ cup olive oil

½ teaspoon kosher salt

½ teaspoon freshly ground black pepper

To make the salad: Combine the watermelon, feta, mint, chives, and arugula in a large bowl. Season with salt.

To make the dressing: Whisk together the red wine vinegar and olive oil in a small bowl. Season with salt and pepper. Drizzle over the watermelon and toss to combine.

Roasted Butternut Squash & Wild Rice Salad

This salad is perfect for anything from a fall dinner party to a work lunch. The longer the salad sits, the better the flavors develop.

Prep time: 20 minutes   Cook time: 45 minutes

FOR THE SALAD

1 cup wild rice, uncooked, rinsed

1 small butternut squash, peeled, seeds removed, and cut into ½-inch pieces

1 red onion, cut into ½-inch-thick slices

2 tablespoons olive oil

1 teaspoon plus 1 teaspoon kosher salt

½ teaspoon plus ½ teaspoon freshly ground black pepper

1 tablespoon fresh tarragon leaves or parsley leaves

FOR THE DRESSING

1½ tablespoons Dijon mustard

3 tablespoons red wine vinegar

1 teaspoon honey

¼ cup olive oil

1 teaspoon kosher salt

½ teaspoon freshly ground black pepper

To make the salad: Preheat the oven to 425°F. Line a baking sheet with foil. Place the wild rice in a pot and cover with 3 cups of water. Bring to a boil then reduce to a simmer and allow to cook until tender, 40 to 45 minutes. Transfer to a large bowl and allow to cool slightly. Meanwhile, place the squash and onions on the baking sheet, drizzle with olive oil, season with 1 teaspoon salt and ½ teaspoon pepper, and toss to coat. Roast until tender and golden, 30 to 35 minutes. Flip the vegetables every 12 to 15 minutes. Add the roasted vegetables and tarragon to the rice. Season with the remaining 1 teaspoon salt and ½ teaspoon pepper.

To make the dressing: Whisk together the mustard, red wine vinegar, and honey in a small bowl. While whisking, slowly drizzle in the olive oil until combined. Season with salt and pepper. Drizzle the dressing over the salad and toss to combine. Serve slightly warm or at room temperature.

Roasted Chickpea Tabbouleh Salad

For a variation, choose your favorite grain to use instead of bulgur!

Prep time: 15 minutes   Cook time: 30 minutes

One 15-ounce can chickpeas, drained and rinsed

2 tablespoons plus 3 tablespoons olive oil

½ teaspoon paprika

1 cup bulgur

1 English cucumber, sliced into ¼-inch half-moons

1 red onion, thinly sliced

½ bunch parsley, leaves removed and roughly chopped

½ bunch mint, leaves removed and roughly chopped

2 tomatoes, diced

1 lemon, juiced

1 teaspoon kosher salt

½ teaspoon freshly ground black pepper

Preheat the oven to 450°F. Place the chickpeas on a baking sheet and pat dry with a paper towel. Drizzle with 2 tablespoons olive oil and sprinkle with paprika. Toss to coat. Roast for 30 minutes until golden and crunchy, tossing halfway through cooking. Remove from the oven and allow to cool. Meanwhile, in a medium saucepan bring the bulgur and 2 cups of water to a boil. Once boiling, cover, reduce to a simmer, and cook until tender, 10 to 12 minutes. Turn off the heat and allow to steam for another 5 to 10 minutes. Remove the lid and fluff with a fork. Transfer the bulgar to a large bowl. Add the cucumber, red onion, parsley, mint, tomatoes, lemon juice, roasted chickpeas, and remaining 3 tablespoons olive oil and toss to combine. Season with salt and pepper.

Tip: If you are pressed for time, skip roasting the chickpeas and add crushed pita chips for extra crunch.

Panzanella Salad with Roasted Chicken

Shop the farmer's market for this salad—what is great about a panzanella is the ability to customize it to whatever is in season or tastes good!

Prep time: 20 minutes   Cook time: 5 minutes

FOR THE SALAD

1 baguette, cut into 1-inch pieces

2 tablespoons olive oil

3 pieces bacon, cooked, and roughly chopped

1 pint cherry tomatoes, halved

½ cup Kalamata olives, pitted

½ red onion, thinly sliced

2 rotisserie chicken breasts, shredded and skin discarded

Basil and shaved Parmesan, for garnish

FOR THE DRESSING

3 tablespoons red wine vinegar

½ cup olive oil

½ teaspoon kosher salt

¼ teaspoon freshly ground black pepper

To make the salad: Preheat the oven to 400°F. Place the bread on a baking sheet and drizzle with olive oil. Bake until toasted and fragrant, 4 to 5 minutes. Remove from the oven and transfer to a large bowl. Add the bacon, cherry tomatoes, olives, red onion, and chicken, and toss to combine.

To make the dressing: Whisk together the red wine vinegar and olive oil in a small bowl, and season with salt and pepper. Pour the dressing around the rim of the large bowl and toss to evenly coat. Garnish with basil and Parmesan. Serve.

Grilled Caesar Wedge Salad

Choose a sturdy lettuce or cabbage when grilling a salad. Grilling is a great option to add new flavors to your favorite salad.

Prep time: 10 minutes   Cook time: 15 minutes

FOR THE SALAD

1 head romaine lettuce, cut into 4 wedges

2 tablespoons plus 2 tablespoons olive oil

½ teaspoon kosher salt

¼ teaspoon freshly ground black pepper

2 slices sourdough or crusty bread, sliced on a bias

1 garlic clove

¼ cup Parmesan cheese, grated

FOR THE DRESSING

3 garlic cloves, minced or pressed

2 teaspoons Dijon mustard

1½ tablespoons mayonnaise

Juice of ½ lemon

¼ teaspoon Worcestershire sauce (optional)

¼ cup olive oil

½ teaspoon kosher salt

¼ teaspoon freshly ground black pepper

To make the salad: Preheat the grill to medium-high heat. Drizzle the romaine wedges with 2 tablespoons olive oil and season with salt and pepper. Place the wedges on the grill and allow to char, 2 to 3 minutes. Flip and allow the other side to char, an additional minute. Transafer the wedges to a platter. Drizzle the bread with the remaining 2 tablespoons olive oil. Place on the grill and toast for 2 minutes per side. Remove from the grill and rub bread with the clove of garlic. Place the bread on the side of salad. Sprinkle the salad with the cheese.

To make the dressing: Whisk together the garlic, mustard, mayonnaise, lemon juice, and Worcestershire in a small bowl. While whisking, slowly drizzle in the olive oil and whisk until well combined. Season with salt and pepper. Drizzle the dressing over salad.

Tip: Instead of whisking, you can place all the salad dressing ingredients in a food processor and pulse to combine.

Charred Green Bean Salad with Warm Bacon Vinaigrette

Say goodbye to soggy steamed green beans! Using a cast-iron skillet or grill pan leaves beans crunchy and flavorful.

Prep time: 10 minutes   Cook time: 15 minutes

2 tablespoons olive oil

3 slices thick-cut bacon

1 small red onion, thinly sliced

1 pound green or yellow beans, ends removed

1 lemon, zested and juiced

½ bunch parsley leaves, roughly chopped

3 tablespoons sherry vinegar or red wine vinegar

1 tablespoon Dijon mustard

½ teaspoon kosher salt

¼ teaspoon freshly ground black pepper

Heat olive oil in a large cast-iron skillet over medium heat. Add the bacon and cook until crispy, 5 to 7 minutes. Transfer the bacon to a paper towel–lined plate and roughly chop. Transfer half of the bacon drippings to a small heatproof bowl. Add the onion to the reserved bacon drippings in the skillet and cook until almost tender, 3 to 4 minutes. Add the beans and cook until charred and crispy, about 5 minutes. Add the lemon juice during the last minute of cooking. Transfer the beans to a large bowl and allow to cool slightly. Add the parsley, lemon zest, and bacon crumbles. Combine the vinegar and mustard in a small bowl. While whisking, slowly add the reserved bacon drippings and season with salt and pepper. Drizzle over the bean salad and toss to combine. Serve warm.

Roasted Beet Salad

Roasting beets in wedges caramelizes the sugars on the outside and also cuts down cooking time.

Prep time: 15 minutes   Cook time: 35 minutes

FOR THE SALAD

1 bunch beets, peeled and cut into ½-inch wedges

2 tablespoons olive oil

½ teaspoon kosher salt

¼ teaspoon freshly ground black pepper

2 cups baby greens

4 ounces blue cheese or goat cheese, crumbled

¼ cup pecans, roughly chopped, for garnish

FOR THE DRESSING

2 tablespoons balsamic vinegar

1 teaspoon honey

¼ cup olive oil

½ teaspoon kosher salt

¼ teaspoon freshly ground black pepper

To make the salad: Preheat the oven to 425°F. Line a baking sheet with foil. Place the beets in a large bowl, drizzle with olive oil, season with salt and pepper, and toss to coat. Transfer the beets to the piece of foil. Bring the edges of the foil together to form a foil packet around the beets. Roast in the oven for 30 to 35 minutes or until tender. Remove from the oven and allow to cool to room temperature. Divide the greens between two plates. Top with the beets and cheese. Drizzle with the honey-balsamic dressing and garnish with pecans.

To make the dressing: Whisk together the balsamic vinegar and honey in a small bowl. While whisking, add the olive oil, and season with salt and pepper.

Orzo Salad with Roasted Tomatoes

Roasting tomatoes brings a charred flavor to the skin and caramelizes the juices—perfect for any pasta, salad, or sandwich.

Prep time: 15 minutes   Cook time: 20 minutes

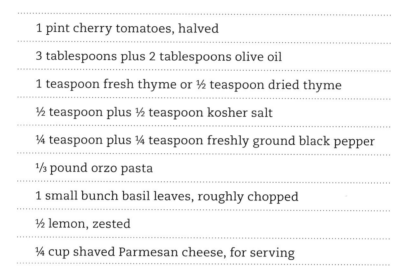

1 pint cherry tomatoes, halved

3 tablespoons plus 2 tablespoons olive oil

1 teaspoon fresh thyme or ½ teaspoon dried thyme

½ teaspoon plus ½ teaspoon kosher salt

¼ teaspoon plus ¼ teaspoon freshly ground black pepper

⅓ pound orzo pasta

1 small bunch basil leaves, roughly chopped

½ lemon, zested

¼ cup shaved Parmesan cheese, for serving

Preheat the oven to 375°F. Line a baking sheet with foil. Place the tomatoes, cut side up on the baking sheet and drizzle with 3 tablespoons of olive oil, sprinkle with thyme, season with ½ teaspoon salt and ¼ teaspoon pepper, and toss to combine. Roast until tender, 15 to 18 minutes. Remove from the oven and allow to cool until slightly warm or room temperature. Meanwhile, cook the orzo according to package instructions until al dente, 7 to 8 minutes. Drain the orzo, transfer to a large bowl, and allow to cool to room temperature. Once the orzo has cooled, add the tomatoes, basil, lemon zest, and remaining 2 tablespoons olive oil, and toss to combine. Season with remaining ½ teaspoon salt and ¼ teaspoon pepper if necessary. Garnish with the shaved Parmesan.

CHAPTER TWO

CHICKEN, BEEF, & PORK

Honey-Lime Chicken Skewers

The perfect recipe for a quick cookout for two during those hot summer months.

Prep time: 20 minutes   Cook time: 15 minutes

12-inch skewers, soaked in water if using wooden skewers

½ pound chicken breast, cut into 1-inch pieces

½ pineapple, skin removed, cored, and cut into 1-inch pieces

2 limes, zested and juiced

1 tablespoon honey

¼ cup olive oil

½ teaspoon cumin

1 serrano pepper, minced

1 teaspoon kosher salt

½ teaspoon freshly ground black pepper

½ teaspoon chili powder

Cilantro, leaves only, for garnish (optional)

Tortillas, warmed, for serving

Thread the chicken pieces onto skewers, about 5 to 6 pieces per skewer. Thread the pineapple pieces onto separate skewers, 5 to 6 pieces per skewer. Combine the lime zest and juice, honey, olive oil, cumin, serrano pepper, salt, and black pepper in a small bowl. Reserve ¼ cup of the marinade in a second bowl. Brush the remaining marinade over the chicken skewers, or place in a zip-top bag with the skewers, and refrigerate for 1 hour. Preheat the grill or grill pan over medium-high heat. Sprinkle the pineapple skewers with chili powder. Place the chicken and pineapple skewers on the grill and cook until charred on all sides, the chicken is cooked through, and the pineapple has caramelized, 3 to 5 minutes per side. Brush the chicken with the reserved marinade halfway through grilling. Remove from the grill and transfer to a platter. Top with cilantro and serve with warm tortillas.

Walnut-Crusted Chicken Breasts with Sautéed Greens

Easy weeknight dinner can happen almost instantly with this recipe. Keep nuts on hand in the freezer and you will never have to worry.

Prep time: 10 minutes   Cook time: 25 minutes

FOR THE CHICKEN

1 tablespoon olive oil

2 boneless, skinless chicken breasts

½ cup panko bread crumbs

½ cup walnuts, finely chopped

2 teaspoons thyme leaves or 1 teaspoon dried thyme

1 teaspoon kosher salt

½ teaspoon freshly ground black pepper

2 tablespoons butter, melted

2 tablespoons Dijon mustard

1 lemon, juiced, plus lemon wedges for serving

FOR THE GREENS

2 tablespoons olive oil

2 cloves garlic, minced

One 8-ounce bag baby spinach

1 teaspoon kosher salt

½ teaspoon freshly ground black pepper

2 teaspoons white wine vinegar

To make the chicken: Preheat the oven to 425°F. Place a baking rack inside of a baking sheet. Heat the olive oil in an heavy-bottomed sauté pan or cast-iron skillet over medium-high heat. Combine the panko, walnuts, thyme, salt, pepper, and butter in a small bowl. Brush the chicken with 1 tablespoon mustard and top with panko mixture, pressing the panko into the chicken. Add the chicken to the sauté pan and cook until golden on both sides, 2 to 3 minutes per side. Transfer the chicken to the baking rack and place it in the oven. Roast until the chicken has reached a temperature of 165°F, 10 to 15 minutes. Shield with foil if the nuts begin to turn too brown.

To make the greens: Heat the olive oil in a large sauté pan or cast-iron skillet over medium-high heat. Add the garlic and cook for 1 minute. Add the spinach, in two batches, tossing until wilted. Season with salt and pepper. Divide the spinich between two plates, drizzle with 1 teaspoon of white wine vinegar, and serve with the chicken with the lemon wedges on the side.

Steak Fajitas

Create that restaurant-style fajita sizzle at home—and enjoy leftovers as another great part of this recipe.

Prep time: 20 minutes   Cook time: 25 minutes

FOR THE MARINADE

1 lime, zested and juiced

1 clove garlic, minced

½ teaspoon cumin

½ teaspoon red chili flakes

½ teaspoon Worcestershire sauce (optional)

1 tablespoon olive oil

1 teaspoon kosher salt

½ teaspoon freshly ground black pepper

FOR THE FAJITAS

¾ pound skirt steak, trimmed

1 red onion, thinly sliced

2 poblano or bell peppers, stems removed, seeded, and thinly sliced

2 tablespoons olive oil

1 teaspoon kosher salt

½ teaspoon freshly ground black pepper

Cilantro leaves, for serving

Lime wedges, for serving

Store-bought pico de gallo, for serving

Flour tortillas, warmed, for serving

Combine all of the marinade ingredients in a large zip-top bag. Add the steak and marinate for 15 minutes at room temperature. Meanwhile, preheat the grill or grill pan to medium-high heat. Place a large cast-iron skillet on the grill. Remove the steak from the marinade and place on the grill. Cook the steak until medium-rare, about 4 minutes per side. Transfer the steak to a cutting board and allow to rest. Place the onions and poblano peppers in a medium bowl and drizzle with olive oil and season with salt and black pepper. Place the vegetables in the cast-iron skillet and cook until charred but not completely tender, 3 to 4 minutes. Remove and keep warm. Slice the steak against the grain into thin slices and serve on a platter with onions, poblano peppers, cilantro, lime wedges, pico de gallo, and tortillas.

Flank Steak with Easy Chimichurri

To make an easy chimichurri, choose your favorite herb and vinegar, mix with olive oil, and enjoy. This dish is perfect to pair with an arugula salad.

Prep time: 5 minutes   Cook time: 10 minutes

FOR THE STEAK

¾ pound flank steak, trimmed

2 teaspoons kosher salt

½ teaspoon freshly ground black pepper

FOR THE CHIMICHURRI

½ cup parsley leaves, roughly chopped

1 garlic clove, minced

2 tablespoons red wine vinegar

¼ cup olive oil

½ teaspoon red chili flakes (optional)

½ teaspoon kosher salt

¼ teaspoon freshly ground black pepper

To make the steak: Preheat the grill or grill pan to medium-high heat. Allow the flank steak to come to room temperature and season both sides with salt and freshly ground black pepper. Place the steak on the grill and cook until medium-rare, 3 to 4 minutes per side. Transfer to a plate, tent with foil to keep warm, and allow to rest before slicing.

To make the chimichurri: Combine the parsley leaves, garlic, red wine vinegar, olive oil, and chili flakes in a medium bowl. Season with salt and pepper.

To serve: Thinly slice the steak against the grain on a bias and top with chimichurri.

Tip: For an even quicker take on chimichurri, buy store-bought pesto and stir in freshly chopped parsley, vinegar, and chili flakes.

Roasted Chicken Thighs with Garlic Potatoes

Sunday roast chicken dinner just became easier and cleaner. With two baking sheets and about 30 minutes of cooking, keep Sunday traditions alive.

Prep time: 15 minutes   Cook time: 35 minutes

FOR THE CHICKEN

2 tablespoons unsalted butter, softened

1 tablespoon fresh or 2 teaspoons dried rosemary leaves, chopped

2 garlic cloves, minced

1 lemon, juiced

4 chicken thighs

3 teaspoons kosher salt

1 teaspoon freshly ground black pepper

1 tablespoon olive oil

FOR THE POTATOES

¾ pound new potatoes, washed, cut in half

3 tablespoons olive oil

2 garlic cloves, minced

2 teaspoons kosher salt

¼ teaspoon freshly ground black pepper

To make the chicken: Preheat the oven to 425°F. Line two baking sheets with foil. Combine the butter, rosemary, garlic, and lemon in a small bowl. Rub the mixture all over the chicken thighs. Season with salt and pepper. Heat the olive oil in a large non-stick sauté pan or cast-iron skillet over medium-high heat. Place the chicken skin-side down and brown on both sides, about 3 minutes per side. Transfer the chicken thighs skin-side up to one of the baking sheets. Place in the oven and roast until the chicken is cooked through and a thermometer reads 165°F, 15 to 20 minutes. Remove from the oven and allow to cool for 5 to 10 minutes.

To make the potatoes: Place the potatoes on the other baking sheet. Drizzle with olive oil and sprinkle evenly with the garlic, salt, and pepper. Toss to evenly coat. Place in the oven with the chicken and allow to roast until tender and golden brown, 20 to 30 minutes, flipping the potatoes every 10 minutes. Remove from the oven and serve with the chicken.

Chicken Tacos with Cilantro Salad

Have your own fiesta with these chicken tacos—with all of this flavor, you may be making this recipe twice in one night!

Prep time: 15 minutes   Cook time: 15 minutes

FOR THE SALAD

3 tablespoons mayonnaise

2 tablespoons white wine vinegar

1 lime, juiced

2 cups shredded cabbage

½ bunch cilantro leaves, roughly chopped

½ red onion, thinly sliced

1 teaspoon kosher salt

½ teaspoon freshly ground black pepper

FOR THE CHICKEN

4 boneless, skinless chicken thighs

1 lime, zested and juiced

½ teaspoon cumin

3 tablespoons olive oil

1 teaspoon kosher salt

½ teaspoon freshly ground black pepper

Four to six 6-inch corn tortillas

Lime wedges for serving

To make the salad: Combine the mayonnaise, white wine vinegar, and lime juice in a large bowl and whisk to combine. Add the cabbage, cilantro, and red onion and toss to evenly coat. Season with salt and pepper. Toss again and set aside.

To make the chicken: Preheat the grill, grill pan, or large cast-iron skillet over medium-high heat. Combine the lime zest and juice, cumin, olive oil, salt, and pepper in a small bowl. Sprinkle the chicken thighs evenly with this seasoning. Place the chicken on the grill and cook until charred and cooked through, 3 to 5 minutes per side, or a thermometer reaches 165°F. Transfer the chicken to a plate to keep warm. Thinly slice. Place the tortillas on the grill and cook until lightly charred and warmed through, about 30 seconds per side. Transfer to a towel to keep warm. Fill the tortillas with a few slices of chicken and top with cilantro salad. Serve with lime wedges.

BBQ Pork Chops with Green Beans & Potatoes

Choose any of your favorite marinades to pair with this recipe. For added flavor, char the pork chops on the grill for 2 minutes per side, then transfer to a baking sheet and cook for 8 to 10 minutes in the oven.

Prep time: 10 minutes   Cook time: 35 minutes

4 boneless pork chops

1 teaspoon plus 1 teaspoon kosher salt

½ teaspoon plus ½ teaspoon freshly ground black pepper

¾ cup favorite store-bought barbecue sauce

2 cups new potatoes, quartered

½ pound green beans, ends trimmed

¼ cup olive oil

4 garlic cloves, minced

Preheat the oven to 375°F. Line 2 baking sheets with foil. Place the pork chops on a baking sheet. Season with 1 teaspoon salt and ½ teaspoon pepper, and coat with barbecue sauce on both sides. Bake until cooked through, 12 to 15 minutes—pork can be slightly pink in the center but should register 145°F on a meat thermometer.

Meanwhile, place the potatoes and green beans on separate sides of a second baking sheet. Drizzle with olive oil and season with remaining 1 teaspoon salt and ½ teaspoon pepper. Toss to coat. Roast until the potatoes and beans are lightly charred and the potatoes are cooked through, 12 to 15 minutes for the beans and 30 to 35 minutes for the potatoes. During the last 10 minutes of the potatoes' cooking time, add the garlic, toss to combine, and return the baking sheet to the oven. Serve the potatoes and green beans with the pork.

Slow Cooker Pulled Pork Sandwiches

Perfect for game day or a cold winter workday. By the time you get home, these sandwiches are ready to put on the table. Pick up some prepared coleslaw to serve on top or on the side of the sandwiches.

Prep time: 15 minutes   Cook time: 5½ hours

2 tablespoons olive oil

1½ pounds boneless pork shoulder

1 tablespoon kosher salt

1 teaspoon freshly ground black pepper

One 12-ounce bottle of lager-style beer or 1½ cups chicken stock

1 poblano pepper, seeded, and thinly sliced

½ red onion, thinly sliced

½ cup store-bought barbecue sauce

2 teaspoons honey

1 tablespoon hot sauce

Four buns, split, for serving

Dill pickle chips, for serving

Heat a large sauté pan with olive oil over medium-high heat. Bring the meat to room temperature and season all sides with salt and the black pepper. Sear the meat in the sauté pan on all sides until browned, 8 to 9 minutes total. Transfer the pork to the bowl of a slow cooker. Deglaze the sauté pan with beer and pour the contents into the slow cooker. Add the poblano pepper and onion to the slow cooker. Cover and cook on low for 5 to 6 hours or until fork tender. When finished cooking, shred the meat using a fork in the slow cooker. Combine the barbecue sauce, honey, and hot sauce in a small bowl.

To serve, place the meat on the bottom bun, spoon over the honey-barbecue sauce, and top with the dill pickles and the top bun.

Mustard-Glazed Pork Tenderloin with Sautéed Apples

Kick pork chops with applesauce up a notch with this mustard-glazed pork tender-loin with roasted apples.

Prep time: 15 minutes   Cook time: 35 minutes

FOR THE TENDERLOIN

2 tablespoons olive oil

One ¾-pound pork tenderloin

1 teaspoon kosher salt

½ teaspoon freshly ground black pepper

2 tablespoons Dijon mustard

2 tablespoons plus ¼ cup whole grain mustard

2 teaspoons light brown sugar

2 teaspoons fresh or 1 teaspoon dried thyme leaves

FOR THE APPLES

3 Granny Smith apples, cored and thinly sliced

2 tablespoons olive oil

½ teaspoon kosher salt

1 teaspoon fresh or ½ teaspoon dried thyme leaves

To make the tenderloin: Preheat the oven to 400°F. Place a baking rack inside of a baking sheet. Heat the olive oil in a large sauté pan or cast-iron skillet over medium-high heat. Season the tenderloin with salt and pepper. Sear the tenderloin on all sides until nicely browned, 6 to 7 minutes. Meanwhile, make the glaze. Combine the Dijon mustard, 2 tablespoons of the whole grain mustard, brown sugar, and thyme leaves in a small bowl. After the tenderloin has been seared, transfer to the baking rack and brush the tenderloin with the glaze. Place in the oven and roast until a meat thermometer reaches 145°F, 20 to 25 minutes. Brush with additional glaze halfway through cooking, if necessary. Remove from the oven and allow to rest for 8 to 10 minutes.

To make the apples: Heat the olive oil in a large sauté pan or cast-iron skillet. Add the apples, season with salt, and cook until almost tender and caramelized, 4 to 5 minutes. Add the thyme during the last minute of cooking.

To serve: Slice the pork tenderloin into ½-inch slices and serve with the apples and ¼ cup of whole grain mustard.

Chicken Lettuce Wraps

Why go out to a Chinese restaurant when you can make these lettuce wraps at home?

Prep time: 15 minutes   Cook time: 25 minutes

FOR THE CHICKEN

2 tablespoons soy sauce

1 tablespoon brown sugar

1 lime, juiced

3 tablespoons olive oil

¼ teaspoon crushed red pepper flakes

2 garlic cloves, smashed

1 teaspoon kosher salt

½ teaspoon freshly ground black pepper

¾ pound boneless, skinless chicken thighs

FOR THE LETTUCE CUPS

1 head bibb lettuce, large leaves removed

¼ cup store-bought matchstick carrots

½ bunch scallions, thinly sliced

Sambal Oelek or other hot sauce, for serving (see note)

Lime wedges, for serving

To make the chicken: Combine all the ingredients in a zip-top bag and allow the chicken to marinate for 15 to 30 minutes at room temperature or up to 2 hours in the refrigerator. When ready to cook, preheat the grill or grill pan to medium-high heat. Remove the chicken from the marinade, discarding any excess marinade, and place the chicken on the grill. Cook until charred on both sides and cooked through, 4 to 5 minutes per side. Roughly chop and tent with foil to keep warm.

To assemble the lettuce cups: Place pieces of bibb lettuce on a platter. Top with chopped chicken, carrots, and scallions. Serve with Sambal Oelek and lime wedges.

Tip: If you can't find Sambal Oelek, substitute Sriracha or any garlic chili sauce you find in the Asian section of your grocery store.

Chicken Sausages with Pickled Cabbage

This is a simple and easy take on a classic German dish.

Prep time: 15 minutes   Cook time: 30 minutes

FOR THE CABBAGE AND SAUSAGES

½ cup apple cider vinegar

2 tablespoons sugar

1 small cabbage, cored and thinly sliced

1 teaspoon kosher salt

½ teaspoon freshly ground black pepper

4 chicken sausages

4 hoagie rolls

FOR THE DIJONNAISE

¼ cup mayonnaise

2 tablespoons Dijon mustard

1 tablespoon fresh or 2 teaspoons dried dill, roughly chopped (optional)

½ teaspoon kosher salt

¼ teaspoon freshly ground black pepper

To make the cabbage: Combine the vinegar and sugar in a medium saucepan over medium heat. Simmer until sugar dissolves, 5 to 6 minutes. Add the cabbage, cover, and simmer until tender, 10 to 12 minutes. Add more water if necessary.

To make the sausages: Preheat the grill or grill pan to medium-high. Add the sausages and cook until charred on all sides and cooked through, 7 to 8 minutes (if you're using raw sausages, check to make sure that they reach 165°F when checked with a meat thermometer). Remove from the heat and keep warm. Place the buns, cut-side down, on the grill to lightly toast. Remove from the grill, spread 1 tablespoon Dijonnaise onto one side of the bun, and top with a sausage and a healthy serving of pickled cabbage.

To make the Dijonnaise: Combine all of the Dijonnaise ingredients in a small bowl.

Turkey Burger Sliders with Spicy Lime Mayonnaise

Upgrade a simple turkey burger with Asian flavors. You can also buy frozen turkey burgers for an even easier weeknight meal.

Prep time: 20 minutes   Cook time: 30 minutes

½ pound ground turkey

2 teaspoons grated ginger

1 garlic clove, minced

1 teaspoon soy sauce

1 teaspoon kosher salt

½ teaspoon freshly ground black pepper

1 lime, juiced

½ cup mayonnaise

1 to 2 teaspoons Sriracha

4 slider buns, toasted

¼ cup cilantro leaves

½ English cucumber, thinly shaved into strips

½ small red onion, thinly sliced

Preheat the grill or grill pan to medium-high heat. (If using a grill pan, heat 2 tablespoons of oil in the pan). Combine the ground turkey, ginger, garlic, soy sauce, salt, and pepper in a large bowl. Form into 4 slider patties. Place the burgers onto the grill and cook until they reach a temperature of 165°F, 4 to 5 minutes per side.

Meanwhile, to make the spicy lime mayonnaise, combine the lime juice, mayonnaise, and Sriracha in a small bowl. Spread 1 to 2 tablespoons of the mayonnaise on the bottom of each slider bun, then top with a turkey burger, cilantro, cucumber, onion, and the top bun.

Chicken Parmesan with Roasted Zucchini

To keep chicken Parmesan simple and healthy, bake in the oven. Serve with roasted zucchini. For quick weeknight meals, bread extra chicken breasts, cook them, and store them in the freezer.

Prep time: 15 minutes   Cook time: 30 minutes

FOR THE CHICKEN

2 tablespoons olive oil

½ cup flour

2 eggs, beaten

1 cup panko bread crumbs

1 teaspoon dried oregano

1 teaspoon garlic powder

4 chicken cutlets

1 teaspoon kosher salt

½ teaspoon freshly ground black pepper

1 cup store-bought garlic-and-basil marinara sauce

1 cup shredded mozzarella cheese

½ cup shredded parmesan cheese

FOR THE ZUCCHINI

2 tablespoons olive oil

2 zucchinis, sliced into ¼-inch rounds

1 teaspoon kosher salt

½ teaspoon freshly ground black pepper

To make the chicken: Preheat the oven to 400°F. Place a baking rack inside of a baking sheet and grease the baking rack with olive oil. Prepare three baking dishes. Place flour in the first; eggs in the second; and panko, oregano, and garlic powder in the third. Season the chicken cutlets with salt and pepper. Dredge the cutlets in flour, shaking off any excess. Dip both sides of each cutlet in the egg mixture and coat in the panko, shaking off any excess. Place the coated chicken cutlets onto the greased baking rack. Bake until the panko is golden and chicken is cooked through, 12 to 15 minutes. Once cooked, remove the chicken from the oven and spoon marinara sauce over the cutlets. Top each cutlet with mozzarella and parmesan cheese. Place chicken back in the oven and bake until the sauce has warmed through and the cheese has melted, 2 to 3 minutes. Serve with the roasted zucchini.

To make the zucchini: Meanwhile, place the zucchini on a second baking sheet. Drizzle with olive oil and season with salt and pepper. Place in the oven and roast until tender, 15 to 20 minutes, flipping halfway through.

Baked Chicken, Bacon, & Pea Risotto

There's no need to continuously stir this risotto; instead, simply bake and enjoy.

Prep time: 15 minutes　Cook time: 1 hour

2 cups plus ½ cup chicken stock

2 slices bacon

½ onion, finely diced

1 teaspoon kosher salt

½ teaspoon freshly ground black pepper

¾ cup arborio rice

¼ cup white wine

1 tablespoon butter

1 cup shredded rotisserie chicken, skin discarded

1 cup frozen peas, thawed

Parmesan cheese, shredded, for serving

Preheat the oven to 350°F. Heat the chicken stock in a small saucepan over medium heat. Heat a small Dutch oven or ovenproof sauté pan with high sides over medium-high heat and cook bacon until crispy, 5 to 7 minutes. Transfer the bacon to a paper towel-lined plate and crumble. Add the onion to the Dutch oven and cook until almost tender, about 5 minutes. Season with salt and pepper. Add the rice and stir to coat in bacon fat. Add the wine and cook until reduced by half, about 3 minutes. Add 2 cups of the chicken stock, cover and place in the oven until rice is al dente, 15 to 20 minutes. Remove from the oven, add the last ½ cup chicken stock, butter, chicken, and peas and return to the oven, uncovered. Bake until the liquid has been absorbed and the chicken is warm, 8 to 10 minutes. Sprinkle the bacon crumbles on top and serve with Parmesan cheese.

Ginger Beef Stir-Fry with Snap Peas

Use a cast-iron skillet to get a good sear on a stir-fry without needing a wok. Serve over white, brown, or fried rice.

Prep time: 25 minutes   Cook time: 15 minutes

¾ pound skirt steak, sliced against the grain ¼-inch thick

3 tablespoons plus 1 tablespoon olive oil

2 tablespoons soy sauce

1 teaspoon honey

1 lime, juiced

1 clove garlic, minced

2 tablespoons ginger, peeled and finely minced or grated

1 teaspoon plus 1 teaspoon kosher salt

½ teaspoon plus ½ teaspoon freshly ground black pepper

½ bunch scallions (white and light green parts only), cut into ½-inch pieces

1 cup snap peas, cut in half

1 cup store-bought matchstick carrots

1 teaspoon sesame seeds, for garnish (optional)

Combine the steak, 3 tablespoons olive oil, soy sauce, honey, lime juice, garlic, and ginger in a baking dish. Cover and marinate for 20 minutes at room temperature. When ready to cook, heat a large cast-iron skillet over medium-high heat. Remove the steak from the marinade, discarding any extra marinade, and place the steak in the skillet. Season with 1 teaspoon salt and ½ teaspoon pepper and cook until medium-rare, 3 to 4 minutes per side. Remove to a plate. Add the remaining olive oil and allow to heat over medium-high heat. Add the scallions, snap peas, and carrots, and cook until slightly charred and almost tender, about 5 minutes. Season with the remaining 1 teaspoon salt and ½ teaspoon pepper. Add the beef back to the skillet. Toss to combine with the vegetables and cook an additional minute. Serve over rice and garnish with sesame seeds, if desired.

Honey Barbecue Baked Chicken Wings

The ultimate game day treat, these chicken wings are a no-hassle sheet pan meal that will make everyone happy.

Prep time: 15 minutes   Cook time: 45 minutes

1 pound chicken wings, tips removed

1 teaspoon kosher salt

½ teaspoon freshly ground black pepper

2 tablespoons olive oil

¾ cup favorite store-bought barbecue sauce

2 tablespoons honey

½ teaspoon cayenne pepper or hot sauce

Chives, sliced, for garnish (optional)

Preheat the oven to 400°F. Line a baking sheet with foil. Place the wings on the baking sheet, season with salt and black pepper, drizzle with olive oil, and toss to combine. Bake for 40 minutes or until the wings are cooked through. Remove from the oven, add the barbecue sauce, drizzle with honey, and sprinkle with cayenne pepper. Toss to combine on the baking sheet and return to the oven to bake until sauce is slightly caramelized, another 5 minutes. Remove and allow to cool slightly, then serve. Garnish with chives.

CHAPTER THREE

SEAFOOD

Blackened Tilapia with Mango Salsa

Use this versatile rub on any type of fish, or even on chicken!

Prep time: 15 minutes   Cook time: 10 minutes

FOR THE FISH

¼ cup store-bought blackened seasoning

2 tilapia fillets, boneless, skinless

2 tablespoons olive oil

1 avocado, peeled, pitted, and thinly sliced (optional)

FOR THE MANGO SALSA

1 mango, skin and pit removed, cut into ½-inch pieces

2 limes, zested and juiced

1 teaspoon honey

½ bunch cilantro leaves

To make the fish: Place the blackened seasoning in a baking dish. Coat the tilapia fillets on both sides with seasoning, shaking off any excess, and place on a plate. Add the olive oil to a large sauté pan or cast-iron skillet and heat over medium-high heat. Add the tilapia fillets and cook until browned on both sides and cooked through, 2 to 3 minutes per side (the fish should flake with a fork).

To make the mango salsa: Combine all of the salsa ingredients in a large bowl. Serve with the blackened fish and sliced avocado.

Shrimp Jambalaya

Bring New Orleans to your kitchen with this easy jambalaya that's full of flavor and spice.

Prep time: 10 minutes   Cook time: 50 minutes

2 tablespoons olive oil

½ pound andouille sausage, sliced into ¼-inch rounds

1 cup fresh or frozen chopped celery, onion, and pepper mix

2 garlic cloves, minced

1 teaspoon paprika

1 teaspoon kosher salt

½ teaspoon freshly ground black pepper

One 15-ounce can plum tomatoes, crushed with hands

2 cups chicken stock

½ cup uncooked long-grain white rice

¾ pound large shrimp, peeled, deveined, tails on

½ bunch scallions, thinly sliced, for garnish

Heat the olive oil in a large Dutch oven or heavy-bottomed skillet over medium-high heat. Add the sausage and cook until browned, about 7 minutes. Transfer the sausage to a paper towel-lined plate. Add the celery, onion, and bell peppers and sauté until almost tender, about 5 minutes. Add the garlic during the last minute of cooking. Add the paprika, salt, and black pepper and stir to combine. Add the tomatoes, chicken stock, and rice and bring to a boil. Lower the heat and allow to simmer until the rice is cooked through, 15 to 20 minutes. Add additional stock if necessary. Add the shrimp and andouille sausage, cover, and allow to cook until the shrimp are pink and opaque, about 10 minutes. Garnish with scallions and serve.

Tip: If you can't find andouille sausage, substitute hot Italian sausage or another spicy pork sausage. Cook the raw sausages through, allow to cool to room temperature, and then slice.

Honey-Mustard
Glazed Salmon

This is the perfect recipe for two or to feed a crowd. The salmon is served with lemony asparagus to complement—be prepared to make extra because everyone will be wanting more.

Prep time: 15 minutes   Cook time: 20 minutes

FOR THE SALMON

2 tablespoons whole grain mustard

1 tablespoon brown sugar

1 teaspoon honey

½ teaspoon kosher salt

½ teaspoon freshly ground black pepper

Two 6-ounce salmon fillets, skin-on, bones removed

FOR THE ASPARAGUS

2 tablespoons olive oil

1 bunch asparagus, woody ends removed

1 pint cherry tomatoes, halved

½ lemon, zested and juiced

½ teaspoon kosher salt

¼ teaspoon freshly ground black pepper

To make the salmon: Preheat the oven to 450°F. Line a baking sheet with foil. Whisk together the mustard, brown sugar, and honey in a small bowl. Season with salt and pepper. Place the salmon fillets on the prepared baking sheet and brush with the glaze. Place in the oven and bake until the salmon is opaque and flaky and the glaze has slightly caramelized, 10 to 15 minutes.

Brush with more glaze halfway through cooking, if necessary. Remove from the oven and serve with the asparagus.

To make the asparagus: Heat the olive oil in a large sauté pan or cast-iron skillet over medium-high heat. Add the asparagus and tomatoes and cook until almost tender but still crisp, about 5 minutes. Add the lemon zest and juice, season with salt and pepper, and toss. Cook an additional minute and serve with the salmon.

Crab Cake Salad

This indulgent classic makes for the perfect date night. Serve crab cakes over salad with your favorite dressing or aioli.

Prep time: 45 minutes   Cook time: 15 minutes

2 tablespoons plus 1 tablespoon olive oil

½ onion, finely diced

1 rib celery, finely diced

1 teaspoon hot sauce

5 tablespoons mayonnaise

½ teaspoon Dijon mustard

¼ cup parsley, finely chopped

1 large egg, lightly beaten

1 teaspoon kosher salt

½ teaspoon freshly ground black pepper

⅓ cup butter crackers, finely crushed

½ pound jumbo lump crab, picked through

1 tablespoon butter

Salad, for serving

Lemon wedges, for serving

Heat 2 tablespoons of olive oil in a sauté pan over medium-high heat. Add the onion and celery and sauté until almost tender, about 5 minutes. Transfer the mixture to a bowl and allow to cool completely. Combine the mayonnaise, Dijon mustard, parsley, and egg in a large bowl. Season with salt and pepper. Add the cooled onion and celery and mix to combine. Add the crackers and gently fold in to combine. Add the crabmeat and gently fold in to combine, without breaking up the lumps. Season again with salt and pepper if necessary. Form the mixture into 4 crab cakes and place on a plate. Cover with plastic wrap and refrigerate for 30 minutes. Heat the butter and remaining 1 tablespoon olive oil in a large non-stick sauté pan over medium-high heat. Add the crab cakes and cook until golden brown and cooked through, about 3 to 4 minutes per side. Remove and serve on top of salad, with lemon wedges on the side.

Shrimp Salad Roll

Perfect for a hot summer day. Use cooked frozen shrimp to cut the time in half. This recipe uses Greek yogurt as a healthier alternative to mayonnaise. If desired, add cucumber, tomato, and lettuce to this sandwich for a fresh crunch.

Prep time: 15 minutes   Cook time: 10 minutes

¾ pound medium shrimp, peeled, deveined, tails removed

½ bunch scallions, thinly sliced on bias

1 stalk celery, finely diced

½ red bell pepper, seeded and finely diced

1 lemon, juiced, plus lemon wedges for serving

½ cup Greek yogurt

1 teaspoon kosher salt

¼ teaspoon freshly ground black pepper

1 tablespoon butter, softened

2 split-top hot dog buns

Lemon wedges, for serving

Bring a large pot of salted water to a boil. Add the shrimp and simmer until cooked through, 3 to 4 minutes. Transfer the shrimp to a paper towel–lined plate and pat dry. Cut the shrimp into bite-sized pieces and transfer to a bowl. Add the remaining ingredients to the shrimp and mix to combine. Season with salt and pepper.

Heat a griddle or nonstick sauté pan over medium-low heat. Spread the butter on the inside of the hot dog buns, place on the griddle, and toast until golden brown, 2 to 3 minutes. Remove the buns from the griddle and top with the shrimp salad. Serve with lemon wedges.

CHAPTER FOUR
VEGETARIAN

Cauliflower Steaks with Lemon Gremolata

Pair this with a small salad or top with the salsa, pesto, or aioli of your choice!

Prep time: 15 minutes   Cook time: 20 minutes

FOR THE CAULIFLOWER

2 tablespoons olive oil

1 head cauliflower, cut into 2-inch steaks

1 teaspoon kosher salt

½ teaspoon freshly ground black pepper

½ teaspoon paprika

½ teaspoon crushed red pepper flakes, for garnish (optional)

FOR THE LEMON GREMOLATA

½ cup parsley leaves, roughly chopped

1 lemon, zested and juiced

1 tablespoon pine nuts, toasted

1 clove garlic, minced

½ teaspoon kosher salt

¼ teaspoon freshly ground black pepper

To make the cauliflower: Preheat the oven to 375°F. Heat the olive oil in a large cast-iron skillet or sauté pan over medium-high heat. Season the cauliflower steaks with salt, black pepper, and paprika. Place in the skillet and cook until golden, about 2 minutes per side. Transfer to a foil-lined baking sheet and roast in the oven until tender, 12 to 14 minutes. Remove the cauliflower from the oven and transfer to a platter. Top with the gremolata and sprinkle with crushed red pepper flakes.

To make the lemon gremolata: Combine all of the gremolata ingredients in a small bowl.

Couscous with Roasted Butternut Squash

This is a delicious fall salad perfect for entertaining guests, bringing to a party, or making for an easy weeknight meal. Serve warm or cold, it's your choice!

Prep time: 15 minutes   Cook time: 30 minutes

3 tablespoons plus 2 tablespoons olive oil

2 cups butternut squash, peeled, seeds removed, cut into ½-inch cubes

1 teaspoon plus 1 teaspoon kosher salt

½ teaspoon plus ½ teaspoon freshly ground black pepper

½ cup vegetable stock

½ cup couscous

2 teaspoons fresh thyme leaves

½ cup goat cheese, crumbled

1 cup baby spinach leaves

Basil leaves, torn, for garnish (optional)

Preheat the oven to 425°F. Line a baking sheet with foil. Place the squash on the baking sheet, toss with 3 tablespoons olive oil, and season with 1 teaspoon salt and ½ teaspoon pepper. Roast until golden and tender, 25 to 30 minutes, flipping halfway through. Remove and allow to cool slightly. Meanwhile, in a medium saucepan add the vegetable stock, season with the remaining 1 teaspoon salt and ½ teaspoon pepper, and bring to a boil. Add the couscous, stir, and remove from the heat. Cover and allow the couscous to soak up all of the liquid, 10 to 15 minutes. Remove the lid and fluff the couscous with a fork. Transfer the couscous to a large bowl and cool slightly. Add the thyme, roasted butternut squash, goat cheese, and spinach and toss to combine. Drizzle with remaining olive oil and garnish with basil leaves, if desired.

Sweet Potato & Refried Bean Tacos

There's no need for meat in tacos when you have this recipe! Hearty and full of flavor, these will appease anyone's cravings.

Prep time: 20 minutes   Cook time: 35 minutes

FOR THE SWEET POTATOES

2 medium sweet potatoes, peeled and ½-inch diced

2 tablespoons olive oil

1 teaspoon chili powder

1 teaspoon kosher salt

½ teaspoon freshly ground black pepper

Six 6-inch corn tortillas, warmed

One 15-ounce can refried beans, warmed

Cilantro leaves, for garnish

FOR THE POBLANO SALSA

1 poblano pepper

2 small ripe tomatoes, diced

½ red onion, finely diced

1 clove garlic, minced

1 lime, juiced

½ teaspoon kosher salt

To make the sweet potatoes: Preheat the oven to 425°F. Line a baking sheet with foil. Add the sweet potatoes to the baking sheet, drizzle with olive oil, and season with chili powder, salt, and black pepper, and toss to combine. Roast until tender and golden, 25 to 30 minutes, flipping halfway through. Remove from the oven and allow to cool slightly. On each warm tortilla add a spoonful of refried beans and top with sweet potatoes and salsa. Garnish with cilantro.

To make the poblano salsa: Preheat the broiler. Place the poblano on a baking sheet under the broiler. Rotate frequently until charred on all sides. Remove from the oven, place in a bowl, cover with plastic wrap, and allow to cool completely. Peel the outer skin off, then remove the seeds and stem and chop. Combine the chopped poblano and the remaining salsa ingredients in a small bowl.

Zucchini & Mushroom Frittata

A gourmet take on breakfast-for-dinner, this frittata is perfect for a quick weeknight dinner or weekend brunch. Serve with arugula salad.

Prep time: 10 minutes   Cook time: 15 minutes

2 tablespoons olive oil

1 cup cremini mushrooms, bottoms of stems trimmed, thinly sliced

1 small zucchini, thinly sliced into half-moons

½ bunch scallions, thinly sliced

2 tablespoons parsley, roughly chopped

2 teaspoons kosher salt

1 teaspoon freshly ground black pepper

6 large eggs, beaten

2 ounces goat cheese, crumbled

1 teaspoon chopped fresh dill, for garnish (optional)

Adjust the oven rack to the top third of the oven and preheat the oven to 350°F. Heat 2 tablespoons of olive oil in an 8-inch ovenproof nonstick sauté pan or cast-iron skillet over medium-high heat. Add the mushrooms, zucchini, and scallions and cook until tender, 5 to 6 minutes. Add the parsley and season with salt and pepper. Add the eggs to the pan, shaking to evenly distribute the mixture. Allow the eggs to set, 3 to 4 minutes. Sprinkle the top of the frittata with goat cheese and place in the oven. Cook until the eggs are just set but slightly jiggle, 6 to 8 minutes. Remove from the oven, loosen the sides with a rubber spatula, and transfer the frittata to a serving plate. Garnish with dill, if desired.

Herbed Macaroni & Cheese

A childhood classic taken up a level with herbs and crunchy corn cereal on top.

Prep time: 25 minutes   Cook time: 40 minutes

FOR THE PASTA

½ pound uncooked macaroni

1 tablespoon plus 2 tablespoons butter

2 tablespoons flour

2 cups whole milk

2 cups sharp cheddar cheese, grated

½ teaspoon paprika

1 teaspoon kosher salt

½ teaspoon freshly ground black pepper

FOR THE TOPPING

1 cup crushed corn cereal or panko bread crumbs

¼ cup Parmesan, grated

2 tablespoons parsley, roughly chopped

2 tablespoons butter, melted

To make the pasta: Preheat the oven to 350°F. Butter an 8-inch square baking dish with 1 tablespoon butter. Bring a large pot of salted water to a boil. Add the pasta and cook for 7 minutes, drain, and set aside. Heat the remaining 2 tablespoons butter in a large pot over medium heat. Once melted, add the flour and whisk to combine, cooking 1 to 2 minutes. Add the milk, whisking constantly. Bring the mixture to a boil, then simmer until thickened, 5 to 7 minutes. Add the cheese, paprika, salt, and pepper. Stir until the cheese is melted. Add the noodles and stir to coat. Transfer the mixture to the baking dish.

To make the topping: Combine the corn cereal, Parmesan, and parsley, in a medium bowl. Drizzle with melted butter then toss to combine. Sprinkle evenly over the noodles and place in the oven. Bake until the cheese is bubbly and the topping is golden brown, 20 to 25 minutes. Remove from the oven, allow to cool for 10 minutes, and serve.

Vegetable Bread Pudding

Perfect for breakfast, lunch, or dinner, add your favorite veggies to this versatile dish.

Prep time: 30 minutes   Cook time: 45 minutes

2 tablespoons olive oil

1½ cups cremini mushrooms, stems removed, thinly sliced

3 cups Swiss chard or kale, stems removed and roughly chopped

¼ cup sun-dried tomatoes in oil, drained and roughly chopped

1 teaspoon plus 1 teaspoon kosher salt

½ teaspoon plus ½ teaspoon freshly ground black pepper

1 tablespoon butter

5 cups day-old sourdough bread, cut into 1-inch chunks

3 eggs

1 cup whole milk

½ cup Parmesan cheese, shredded

Heat the olive oil in a large sauté pan over medium-high heat. Add the mushrooms and cook until tender, about 5 minutes. Add the Swiss chard in batches and cook until wilted. Add the sun-dried tomatoes and stir to combine. Season with 1 teaspoon salt and ½ teaspoon pepper. Remove from the heat and allow to cool to room temperature.

Preheat the oven to 350°F. Butter an 8-inch square baking dish and place the bread cubes inside. Evenly top with the mushroom mixture. Whisk the eggs, milk, and Parmesan together in a large bowl. Season with remaining 1 teaspoon salt and ½ teaspoon pepper. Pour over the bread and press the bread down to coat in liquid. Soak for 15 to 20 minutes. Cover with foil and bake for 25 minutes, then uncover and bake until puffed and golden brown with a slight jiggle, another 10 to 15 minutes. Allow to cool for 10 minutes before serving.

Portobello Burgers

Perfect for dinner or a party appetizer, this recipe is a crowd-pleaser.

Prep time: 10 minutes   Cook time: 15 minutes

FOR THE BURGERS

1 clove garlic, minced

2 tablespoons plus 1 tablespoon olive oil

1 red bell pepper, stem removed, seeds discarded, cut into quarters

½ teaspoon plus 1 teaspoon kosher salt

½ teaspoon plus ½ teaspoon freshly ground black pepper

2 portobello mushrooms, stems removed

2 wheat buns, split and toasted

1 cup baby arugula

¼ cup feta, crumbled

FOR THE BALSAMIC AIOLI

2 tablespoons mayonnaise

1 teaspoon balsamic vinegar

1 teaspoon olive oil

To make the burgers: Preheat the grill or grill pan over medium-high heat. Place a cast-iron skillet on the grill or stove and heat over medium-high heat. Combine the garlic, 2 tablespoons olive oil, and red bell pepper in a large bowl. Season with 1/2 teaspoon salt and 1/2 teaspoon black pepper. Add the bell peppers to the cast-iron skillet and cook until charred and tender, 5 to 7 minutes. Remove and set aside. Brush the mushrooms with remaining 1 tablespoon olive oil and season with 1 teaspoon salt and 1/2 teaspoon black pepper. Place on the grill and allow to cook until charred and tender, about 3 minutes per side. Transfer the mushrooms to a plate.

Spread 1 tablespoon of balsamic aioli on the bottom bun, top with half the argula, a portobello mushroom, half of the bell peppers, and the feta. Place top bun on top and serve.

To make the balsamic aioli: Combine the mayonnaise, balsamic vinegar, and olive oil in a small bowl.

Vegetarian Nachos with Corn & Black Beans

Sometimes you just need a cheat night. These nachos are the perfect solution.

Prep time: 15 minutes   Cook time: 5 minutes

½ bag restaurant-style tortilla chips

½ red onion, finely diced

One 15-ounce can black beans, drained and rinsed

½ cup corn kernels, removed from the cob or frozen and thawed

½ teaspoon cumin

1 teaspoon kosher salt

½ teaspoon freshly ground black pepper

2 cups Mexican blend shredded cheese

2 tomatoes, diced

¼ cup pickled jalapeños, chopped

1 avocado, pitted, peeled, and diced

Sour cream, for serving

Preheat the broiler. Combine the tortilla chips, red onion, black beans, corn, cumin, salt, and black pepper in an 8-inch square baking dish. Evenly scatter the cheese over the top and place under the broiler. Cook until the cheese is melted and bubbly, 3 to 4 minutes. Remove from the oven and top with tomatoes, pickled jalapenos, and avocado and serve with sour cream on the side.

CHAPTER FIVE

ONE-POT MEALS

Beef Chili with Poblanos

Freeze this recipe in batches to always have a last-minute weeknight dinner on hand.

Prep time: 15 minutes   Cook time: 45 minutes

2 tablespoons olive oil

¾ pound ground sirloin

1 red onion, diced

2 poblano peppers, stems removed, seeded, and diced

2 garlic cloves, minced

1 teaspoon cumin

3 teaspoons chili powder

½ cup lager-style beer

One 15-ounce can diced tomatoes

1 cup beef broth

One 15-ounce can kidney beans, drained and rinsed

2 teaspoons kosher salt

½ teaspoon freshly ground black pepper

Scallions, thinly sliced, for serving

Sour cream, for serving

Cheddar cheese, grated, for serving

Heat the olive oil in a large heavy-bottomed pot or Dutch oven over medium-high heat. Add the beef and cook until browned, 7 to 9 minutes. Add the onion and poblano peppers and cook until almost tender, about 4 minutes. Add the garlic during the last minute of cooking. Add the cumin and chili powder, stir to combine, and cook until aromatic. Deglaze the pan with beer and bring to a boil. Add the tomatoes, beef broth, and beans, bring to a boil, and then reduce to a simmer and cook for 30 minutes. Season with salt and black pepper. Serve with scallions, sour cream, and cheddar cheese.

Chicken & Corn Chowder

The perfect solution to a cold winter night. Serve with warm, crusty bread.

Prep time: 20 minutes   Cook time: 35 minutes

1 tablespoon olive oil

3 slices bacon, roughly chopped

½ onion, chopped

2 stalks celery, chopped

2 garlic cloves, minced

2 tablespoons flour

1 cup milk

1 teaspoon fresh thyme leaves

1½ cups new potatoes, halved

2½ cups chicken stock

1 teaspoon kosher salt

½ teaspoon freshly ground black pepper

½ rotisserie chicken, shredded and skin discarded

1 cup corn, freshly removed from the cob, or frozen and thawed

2 slices white bread, cut into ½ inch cubes and toasted

Parsley, roughly chopped, for garnish (optional)

Heat the oil in a large heavy-bottomed pot over medium-high heat. Add the bacon and cook until crispy, 5 to 7 minutes. Transfer the bacon to a paper towel-lined plate. Add the onion and celery and cook until almost tender, about 5 minutes. Add the garlic during the last minute of cooking. Add the flour and stir to coat, cooking for 1 minute. Whisk in the milk and bring to a boil, reduce to a simmer and allow to thicken, 4 to 5 minutes. Add the thyme, potatoes, chicken stock, salt, and pepper, and bring to a boil, then reduce to a simmer, cover, and cook until potatoes are tender, 12 to 15 minutes, adding more chicken stock if necessary. Add the chicken and corn and simmer until warmed through, about 5 minutes. Top with toasted bread croutons and garnish with parsley.

Chickpea & Sweet Potato Coconut Curry

Packed with protein and flavor, this dish is perfect to prepare during a busy week with minimal time for cooking.

Prep time: 15 minutes   Cook time: 40 minutes

2 tablespoons olive oil

½ onion, finely diced

½ bell pepper, seeded and diced

1 clove garlic, minced

2 teaspoons ginger, peeled and grated

2 teaspoons curry powder

1 teaspoon kosher salt

½ teaspoon freshly ground black pepper

1 plum tomato, small diced

Half of 13- to 15-ounce can coconut milk

One 15-ounce can chickpeas, drained and rinsed

1 large sweet potato, peeled, cut into ½-inch cubes

1 cup cooked long grain white rice, for serving

¼ cup roasted and salted cashews, for garnish

Heat the olive oil in a large sauté pan over medium-high heat. Add the onion, bell pepper, garlic, and ginger and cook until the onion is tender, 4 to 5 minutes. Add the curry powder, salt, and pepper and cook an additional minute. Add the tomato and coconut milk, mix to combine. Add the chickpeas and sweet potatoes, bring to a boil then lower the heat to a simmer, cover, and cook until the sweet potatoes are tender, 25 to 30 minutes. Serve over white rice and garnish with cashews.

White Bean Stew with Kale

Hearty for a cold winter day, use any beans with this stew and add bacon if desired. Serve with crusty bread.

Prep time: 15 minutes   Cook time: 40 minutes

2 tablespoons olive oil

1 onion, small diced

1 carrot, peeled and roughly chopped

1 stalk celery, roughly chopped

1 clove garlic, minced

2 teaspoons fresh or 1 teaspoon dried thyme

¼ teaspoon crushed red pepper flakes

1 teaspoon kosher salt

½ teaspoon freshly ground black pepper

1 bunch kale, stems removed, roughly chopped into 1-inch pieces

3 cups vegetable broth

One 15-ounce can diced tomatoes

One 15-ounce can cannellini beans, drained and rinsed

Crusty bread, for serving

Heat the olive oil in a large pot over medium-high heat. Add the onion, carrot, and celery and cook until almost tender, about 4 minutes. Add the garlic, thyme, crushed red pepper flakes, salt, and black pepper, and cook for an additional minute. Add the kale and cook until wilted, about 4 minutes. Add the broth and diced tomatoes, bring to a simmer, and simmer for 20 minutes. During the last 10 minutes of cooking, add the beans and continue to simmer. Season with salt and pepper, if desired. Ladle into bowls and serve with crusty bread.

Beef & Vegetable Stew

Stay warm and full with this comforting classic. Better yet, you only need one pot to cook this meal. Add your favorite root vegetables for a stew full of flavor.

Prep time: 15 minutes   Cook time: 1 hour 45 minutes

2 tablespoons olive oil

2 pounds boneless beef chuck roast, cut into 1-inch pieces

1 teaspoon kosher salt

½ teaspoon freshly ground black pepper

½ cup flour

1 small onion, diced

2 carrots, peeled and sliced ½ inch thick

1 rib celery, roughly chopped

2 garlic cloves, minced

1 teaspoon fresh or ½ teaspoon dried thyme

1 tablespoon tomato paste

1 cup lager-style beer (optional—add an additional 1 cup of beef stock if not using)

2 cups beef stock

2 cups baby Yukon Gold potatoes, halved or quartered

Heat the olive oil in a large heavy-bottomed pot or Dutch oven over medium-high heat. Season the beef with salt and pepper. Place the flour in a baking dish and coat the beef on all sides, shaking off any excess. Add the beef to the pot and brown on all sides, 7 to 8 minutes, and transfer to a plate. Add the onion, carrots, and celery to the pot and cook until lightly browned and almost tender, about 5 minutes. Add the garlic and thyme during the last minute of cooking. Add the tomato paste and cook, stirring to coat the vegetables, for 1 to 2 minutes. Deglaze the pan with beer and reduce slightly. Add the beef stock and beef to the pot, bring to a boil, and reduce to a simmer. Allow to cook until meat is tender, about 1½ hours. Add the potatoes during the last 30 minutes of cooking. Season with additional salt and pepper if desired.

Skillet Chicken Potpie

Use leftover chicken and store-bought biscuit dough for this easy skillet potpie.

Prep time: 10 minutes   Cook time: 30 minutes

2 tablespoons butter

¾ cup fresh or frozen chopped onion, carrot, and celery mix

1 clove garlic, minced

2 teaspoons rosemary, leaves chopped

1 teaspoon kosher salt

½ teaspoon freshly ground black pepper

2 tablespoons flour

1 cup chicken stock

½ cup whole milk

2 rotisserie chicken breasts, shredded and skin discarded

½ cup frozen peas and corn, thawed

1 can store-bought biscuit dough

Preheat the oven to 350°F. In an 8-inch cast-iron skillet, add the butter and heat over medium-high heat. Add the onion, carrots, and celery and cook until almost tender, about 5 minutes. Add the garlic and rosemary during the last minute of cooking. Season with salt and pepper. Add the flour, stirring to the coat vegetables. Add the chicken stock, bring to a simmer, and allow to thicken slightly, 5 to 7 minutes. Add the milk and stir to combine. Add the chicken, peas, and corn and stir to combine. Place the biscuit rounds on top of the chicken mixture and place in the oven to cook until golden brown, 12 to 15 minutes. Cover with foil if the biscuits are browning too quickly. Remove and cool for 10 minutes before serving.

Baked Penne with Ricotta

Cut out the hours it takes to make baked rigatoni with this one-pot recipe—half the time and half the mess!

Prep time: 5 minutes   Cook time: 30 minutes

4 ounces hot Italian sausage, removed from casing

2 garlic cloves, minced

2 teaspoons tomato paste

Two 15-ounce cans stewed tomatoes

6 ounces uncooked penne or rigatoni

1½ cups water

½ cup mozzarella cheese, grated

½ cup fresh ricotta

2 tablespoons basil, roughly chopped, for garnish (optional)

Preheat the broiler. Heat the olive oil in a heavy-bottomed Dutch oven or sauté pan with high sides over medium-high heat. Add the sausage and cook, breaking into crumbles with the back of a wooden spoon until browned all over, 6 to 7 minutes. Add the garlic and tomato paste and cook an additional minute. Add the stewed tomatoes, bring to a simmer, and allow to thicken, 5 to 7 minutes. Add the uncooked penne and water, bring to a boil and reduce to a simmer, and cook the pasta until al dente, 8 to 10 minutes. Remove the pan from the heat and stir in half of the mozzarella cheese. Top with dollops of ricotta and evenly sprinkle the remaining mozzarella on top. Place under the broiler until the cheese is bubbling and golden brown, 2 to 3 minutes. Remove from the oven and garnish with basil.

Vegetable Fried Rice

The perfect no-hassle dish for any leftover rice and veggies in the fridge.

Prep time: 10 minutes   Cook time: 15 minutes

2 tablespoons olive oil

2 green bell peppers, stems removed, seeded, cut into ½-inch strips

1 pound cremini mushrooms, stems removed, thinly sliced

1 cup snow peas

1 clove garlic, minced

1 cup scallions, thinly sliced and divided into two portions

½ teaspoon kosher salt

¼ teaspoon freshly ground black pepper

2 cups cooked long grain white rice

2 eggs, beaten

2 tablespoons soy sauce

Heat the olive oil in a large sauté pan over medium-high heat. Add the bell peppers, mushrooms, snow peas, garlic, and half of the scallions and cook until the peppers and mushrooms are almost tender, 3 to 4 minutes. Season with salt and black pepper. Add the rice and stir to combine. Cook the rice until almost crispy, about 2 minutes. Move the rice and vegetables to one side of the sauté pan and add the eggs to the other. Cook the eggs while mixing into the rice mixture to incorporate. Add the soy sauce and mix to combine. Top with remaining scallions and serve.

Chicken Enchiladas

Fiesta night in a flash any day of the week! These enchiladas are stacked to make a casserole that is easier and quicker to assemble than traditional rolled enchiladas.

Prep time: 10 minutes   Cook time: 20 minutes

Four 6-inch corn tortillas

2 tablespoons olive oil

½ red onion, finely diced

1 garlic clove, minced

2 cups shredded rotisserie chicken, skin discarded

1 teaspoon kosher salt

½ teaspoon freshly ground black pepper

One 15-ounce can black beans, drained and rinsed

1 cup frozen corn, thawed and divided into two ½-cup portions

½ teaspoon plus ½ teaspoon cumin

1 lime, juiced, divided in half

One 15-ounce can diced tomatoes, divided in half

1 cup enchilada sauce, divided in half

2 cups shredded pepper Jack cheese, divided in thirds

Sour cream, for serving

Preheat the oven to 350°F. Char the corn tortillas in a dry 10- or 12-inch cast-iron skillet or over an open flame on a gas stove, using caution. Remove from the stove and allow the tortillas to cool. Heat the olive oil in the cast-iron skillet or a deep nonstick sauté pan over medium-high heat. Add the onion and cook until almost tender, about 5 minutes. Add the garlic and continue to cook for 1 minute. Add the chicken and black beans and cook until warmed through, about 4 minutes. Season with salt and pepper and remove half of this mixture to a bowl. Add half of the corn, cumin, lime juice, tomatoes, and enchilada sauce to the skillet. Sprinkle with ⅓ of the pepper Jack cheese. Layer two of the tortillas on top. Top with the remaining chicken mixture, corn, cumin, lime juice, tomatoes, enchilada sauce, ⅓ of the cheese, and remaining two corn tortillas. Top with remaining ⅓ of the cheese, cover with foil, and bake in the oven until warmed through and the cheese has melted, 10 to 15 minutes. Remove from the oven and serve with sour cream on the side.

Squash Bake with Goat Cheese

Perfect for a weekend brunch or lunch, use whatever produce is in season for this bake. This recipe makes two meal-sized portions or four side portions.

Prep time: 15 minutes   Cook time: 25 minutes

2 tablespoons plus 2 tablespoons olive oil

3 zucchini, sliced ¼ inch thick, divided in half

3 summer squash, sliced ¼ inch thick, divided in half

1 tablespoon fresh or 2 teaspoons dried thyme

1 teaspoon kosher salt

1 teaspoon freshly ground black pepper

1 cup Monterey Jack cheese, shredded, divided in half

½ cup panko bread crumbs

4 ounces goat cheese, crumbled

2 tablespoons chopped chives, for garnish (optional)

Preheat the oven to 375°F. Grease an 8-inch square baking dish with 2 tablespoons olive oil. Toss the squash with remaining 2 tablespoons of olive oil, thyme, salt, and pepper. Layer half of the squash in the baking dish, and top with half of the thyme and the Monterey Jack cheese. Repeat. Sprinkle bread crumbs on top. Bake until squash is almost tender and cheese is bubbling and golden brown, 20 to 25 minutes. Remove from the oven and sprinkle with goat cheese, then return to the oven and bake until the goat cheese is warmed, about 4 minutes. Garnish with chives, if desired.

Mexican Rice
Casserole

A fiesta in one pot! No need to have the hassle of tacos with a thousand toppings—just make this easy rice casserole with all of your favorite taco ingredients. This is the perfect dish to use leftover chicken.

Prep time: 10 minutes   Cook time: 40 minutes

2 tablespoons olive oil

2 chicken breasts, cut into 1-inch pieces

1 teaspoon plus 1 teaspoon kosher salt

½ teaspoon plus ½ teaspoon freshly ground black pepper

1 red onion, diced

1 jalapeño, thinly sliced

2 cloves garlic, minced

1½ teaspoons cumin

2 cups short grain white rice

One 15-ounce can diced tomatoes

4 cups chicken stock

One 15-ounce can black beans, drained and rinsed

1 cup frozen corn, thawed

Cheddar cheese, grated, for serving

Heat the olive oil in a large, deep sauté pan or shallow pot over medium-high heat. Season the chicken with 1 teaspoon salt and ½ teaspoon black pepper. Add the chicken to the pan and cook until browned on all sides and cooked through, 7 to 9 minutes. Transfer the chicken to a plate. Add the onion and jalapeño to the pan and cook until the onion is almost tender, about 4 minutes. Add the garlic and cumin during the last minute of cooking. Season with remaining 1 teaspoon salt and ½ teaspoon pepper. Add the rice and tomatoes and cook for 2 minutes. Add the chicken stock, bring to a boil, then reduce to a simmer. Cover and simmer until the rice is almost cooked through, 15 to 17 minutes. Add the black beans, corn, and chicken and continue to cook until the rice is tender and the beans are warmed through, 5 to 7 minutes. Serve with cheddar cheese.

Index

meat. *See* beef; chicken; pork; turkey

Mexican Rice Casserole, 120–21

mint

Roasted Chickpea Tabbouleh Salad, 22–23

Watermelon Salad with Feta &, 18–19

Monterey Jack cheese, in Squash Bake with Goat Cheese, 118–19

mozzarella cheese

Baked Penne with Ricotta, 112–13

Caprese Salad with Basil Pesto, 16–17

Chicken Parmesan with Roasted Zucchini, 60–61

mushrooms

Vegetable Bread Pudding, 92–93

Vegetable Fried Rice, 114–15

Zucchini & Mushroom Frittata, 88–89

Mustard-Glazed Pork Tenderloin with Sautéed Apples, 52–53

N

Nachos with Corn & Black Beans, Vegetarian, 96–97

nuts. *See* walnuts

O

one-pot meals, 99–121

Baked Penne with Ricotta, 112–13

Beef Chili with Poblanos, 100–101

Beef & Vegetable Stew, 108–9

Chicken & Corn Chowder, 102–3

Chicken Enchiladas, 116–17

Chickpea & Sweet Potato Coconut Curry, 104–5

Mexican Rice Casserole, 120–21

Skillet Chicken Pot Pie, 110–11

Squash Bake with Goat Cheese, 118–19

Vegetable Fried Rice, 114–15

White Bean Stew with Kale, 106–7

Orzo Salad with Roasted Tomatoes, 32–33

P

Panzanella Salad with Roasted Chicken, 24–25

parmesan cheese, in Chicken Parmesan with Roasted Zucchini, 60–61

peas

Baked Chicken, Bacon, & Pea Risotto, 62–63

Ginger Beef Stir-Fry with Snap Peas, 64–65

snow peas, in Vegetable Fried Rice, 114–15

Penne with Ricotta, Baked, 112–13

Pepper Jack cheese, in Chicken Enchiladas, 116–17

pesto, in Caprese Salad with Basil Pesto, 16–17

pineapple, in Honey-Lime Marinated Chicken Skewers, 36–37

Poblano Salsa, 86–87

pork

BBQ Pork Chops with Green Beans & Garlic Potatoes, 48–49

Mustard-Glazed Pork Tenderloin with Sautéed Apples, 52–53

Slow Cooker Pulled Pork Sandwiches, 50–51

Portabella Burgers, 94–95

potatoes

Beef & Vegetable Stew, 108–9

Chicken & Corn Chowder, 102–3

Garlic Potatoes, BBQ Pork Chops with Green Beans &, 48–49

Garlic Potatoes, Roasted Chicken Thighs with, 44–45

Pot Pie, Skillet Chicken, 110–11